READING POWER

Marion Jones
World-Class Runner
Heather Feldman

The Rosen Publishing Group's
PowerKids Press ™
New York

1

For Sophie Megan

Published in 2001 by The Rosen Publishing Group, Inc.
29 East 21st Street, New York, NY 10010

First Edition

Book Design: Michael de Guzman

Photo Credits: pp. 5, 19 © CLIVE MASON/ALLSPORT; p. 7 © MIKE POWELL/ ALLSPORT; p. 9 © Rob Tringali Jr./SportsChrome; pp. 11, 17 © Bongarts Photography/SportsChrome; p.13 © DOUG PENSINGER/ALLSPORT; pp. 15, 21 © GARY M. PRIOR/ALLSPORT.

Feldman, Heather.
    Marion Jones : world-class runner / Heather Feldman.
      p. cm.— (Reading power)
    Includes index.
    Summary: Simple text and photographs describe the achievements of a world-class runner.
    ISBN 0-8239-5718-7
    1. Jones, Marion, 1975– —Juvenile literature. 2. Runners (Sports)—United States—Biography—Juvenile literature. 3. Women runners—United States— Biography—Juvenile literature. [1. Jones, Marion, 1975– 2. Track and field athletes. 3. Women—Biography. 4. Afro-Americans—Biography.] I. Title. II. Series.

GV1061.15.J67 F46 2000
796.323'092—dc21   00-036710
[B]

Manufactured in the United States of America

Contents

Marion Jones is a runner.
Marion runs fast.

Marion works hard at being a fast runner. She sprints around the track.

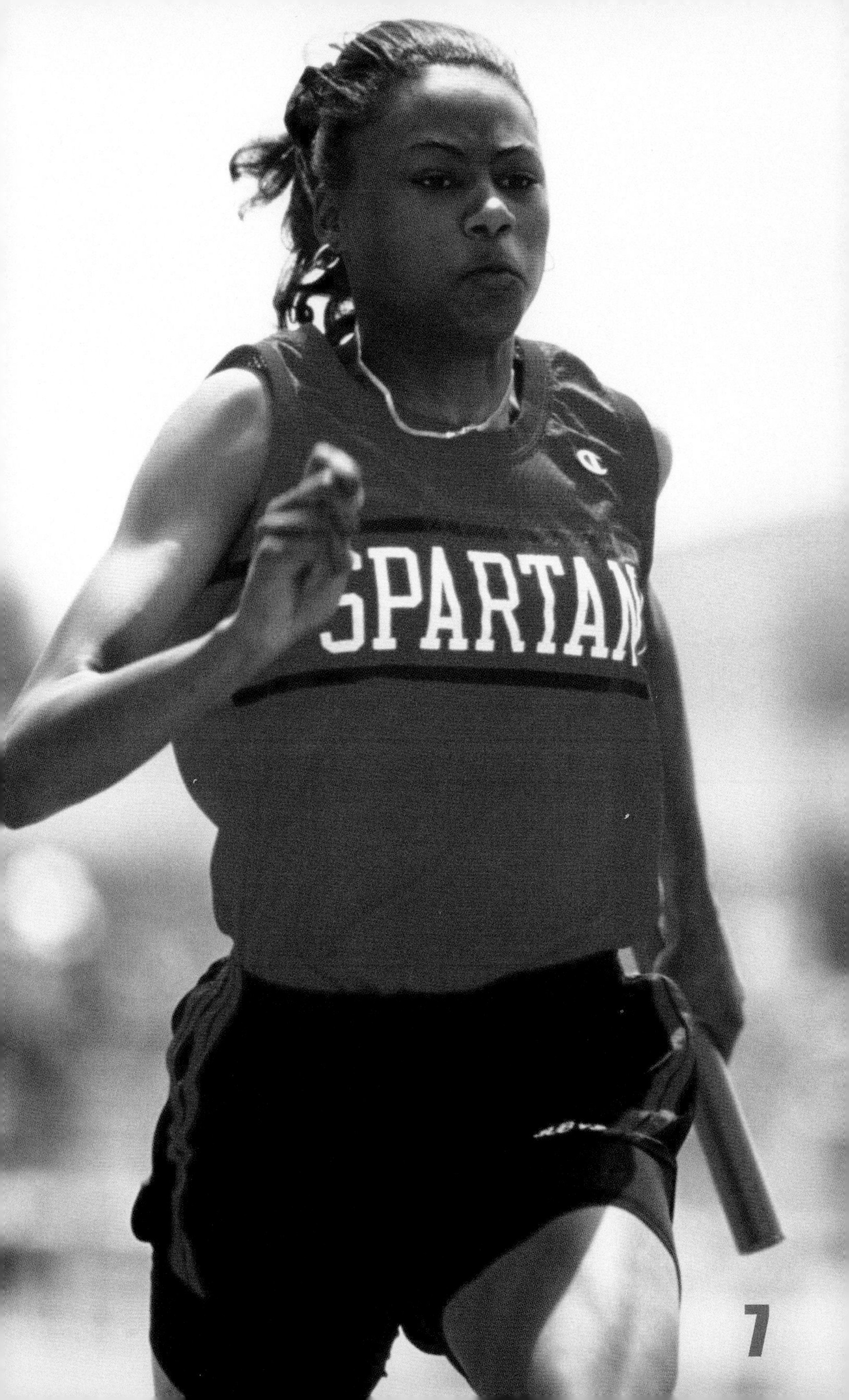
SPARTAN

Marion works out to stay in shape. Staying in shape helps Marion run fast.

9

Marion is also a great jumper. Marion jumps high.

Marion played basketball, too. She played basketball in college. Marion is a great athlete.

Marion gets flowers when she wins a race. Marion wins a lot of races. Marion is one of the best runners in the world.

15

Marion gets a medal when she wins a race. She kisses the medal. Marion is happy when she runs well.

Marion has a lot of fans.
She waves to her fans.

19

Marion runs for the United States. She wins medals for the United States. She likes to win. Most of all, Marion likes to run!

Glossary

athlete (ATH-leet) A person who takes part in sports.

jumper (JUM-per) A person that jumps.

sprints (SPRIHNTZ) To run at top speed for a
   short distance.

track (TRAK) The place where runners practice and
   race.

Here is another good book to read about Marion Jones:

Marion Jones: Sprinting Sensation
(Sports Stars)
by Mark Stewart
Children's Press (1999)

To learn more about running, check out this Web site:

http://www.yahooligans.com/Sports _and_Recreation/Track_and_Field/

Index

Word Count: 137

Note to Librarians, Teachers, and Parents

If reading is a challenge, Reading Power is a solution! Reading Power is perfect for readers who want high-interest subject matter at an accessible reading level. These fact-filled, photo-illustrated books are designed for readers who want straightforward vocabulary, engaging topics, and a manageable reading experience. With clear picture/text correspondence, leveled Reading Power books put the reader in charge. Now readers have the power to get the information they want and the skills they need in a user-friendly format.